Cleave

Anne O'Connell

SUMMER PALACE PRESS

First published in 2023 by

Summer Palace Press
Cladnageeragh, Kilbeg, Kilcar, County Donegal, Ireland
and
Pegasus, 137 Ballantine Gardens, Hillhall Road,
Ballymullan, Lisburn, County Antrim BT27 5FJ

Printed by W&G Baird Ltd

ISBN: 978-0-9954529-8-5

This book is printed on elemental chlorine-free paper

for Clara, Emma, my grandson Philip
and my partner Michael

Acknowledgements

Some of these poems have appeared in: *The Stinging Fly*; *Riposte*; *The Stony Thursday Book*; *Cyphers*; *Writing from Roscommon*; *Aesthetica*; *Badal*; *The International Library of Poetry*; *Dolly Mixtures* and *Mid-Life Slices*, published in 2012 to raise funds for the Cancer Support Centre in Sligo.

Biography

Anne O'Connell was born in Donegal and lives in County Sligo. She trained as a Montessori teacher and was employed in Special Education before retraining as a psychotherapist. Many of her poems have been published in journals and anthologies, and in 2018 she produced *Standing in the Footprints*, edited by Ted and Annie Deppe, with her poems accompanied by the photographs of Michael McCormick. From 2005 to 2014 Anne and Michael had collaborated on the production of the annual Sligo Poets' calendar.

Prior to that she had attended the Poets' House, Falcarragh, County Donegal, and attained an M.A. in Creative Writing from Lancaster University in 2002. In 2012 she trained as a Creative Writing facilitator in Amherst, Massachusetts.

Anne has held a Sligo County Council residency at the Tyrone Guthrie Centre, Annaghmakerrig and her work has been broadcast on *RTE Radio* and on Brian Leyden's series *The Third Sunday* on *Ocean FM*. She has given readings at various venues including the Allingham Festival, where she won second prize.

Her poems have been shortlisted in *The Sunday Tribune* Hennessey Awards; the Yeats Poetry Competition; the North-West Words Aurivo International Poetry Competition and she was the winner of the Kerry Arts Festival *Samhlaíoch Chiarraí*.

Contents

The Photograph

You stand together on the dance floor
waiting for the next song,
young lovers full of promise,
white embroidered flowers
on the bodice of your 1950s dress.

Caught in a charming smile
he seems so clean-cut, innocent.

You are not burdened yet
with children, daughter after daughter,
or weighted with the worry
of his next drinking bout.

You haven't found the lump,
don't know life will be so short.

Legacy

You gave me journeys cramped in the back
of a Volkswagen beetle. Childhood,
sea swims, family picnics.

You gave me summer work, long hours,
early mornings, hotel visitors, customers,
low wages.

You gave me dances, showbands,
the Hippy Hippy Shake, a Singer sewing machine
to make mini-skirts and bell-bottoms.

You gave me birthday gifts,
a brown leather shoulder bag, no card,
an embossed silver mirror, handshakes,
no hug.

You gave me horses, racing greyhounds,
thoroughbreds, highly strung,
suspicion about secretive gambling.

You left books on architecture,
houses in your head that you never built
but a home that you did.

A home with long, stained-glass
window, a sea view,
an under-the-stairs study.

You left me in silence, without conversation,
with unanswered questions.
You left me worrying on the days you drank.

You left your brothers, a sister,
your wife, daughters. You left.
You left me bereft.

It's a Dog's Life

Even when they ate
the upholstery
inside the doors of his jeep
he wasn't angry with them:

they were doing what dogs do
when bored or left alone
without the man they love
and have no way of knowing

if he will ever come back
and take them on his knee,
flattening their ears
with a stroke of his hand.

They will sniff
the air, raise their ears
to the sound of his step,
see him through the window,

turning the key,
opening the door. A heap
of flittered leatherette
falls down at his feet!

Teddy

The one she got attached to
was the pink bear
because she held him
while the tests were being done,

when her mother had to leave,
when they woke her in the night
to check her temperature,
when other children cried.

When her parents brought her home
she stuck the knitting needle
in him and said *relax*
just like the doctors did in hospital.

Warmth of Remembering

Every time I climb the stairs for bed,
I pass the ceramic pot, its hand-painted pattern
blue and yellow, a bargain she found
in a local junk shop. It will always say
Happy Birthday.

Happy Christmas is the grey settee cushion
embroidered with reindeer.
Postcards from her journeys –
Dubai, Arizona, Las Vegas, Sicily…

I wrap the long green cardigan around me
on a winter's day, for the warmth of remembering
her gift packages on the porch mat.
Now, I visit her grave: *In Loving Memory*
inscribed on a granite headstone.

Letting go is not a one-off event.

Bouncing on Maple

It was cool in the sixties to hold a cigarette
between your fingers even if you didn't smoke.
Cooler still if you wore false eyelashes
thick with black mascara, and backcombed your hair
to create a bouffant effect.

The perfume was *Midnight*, applied to the wrists
and behind the ears, the final touch
before heading for the dancehall.
No alcohol allowed, only relevant
to men back then.

Two sips of *Babycham* would set a girl
giggling and dizzy as the nymph
on the champagne glass she drank from.
In any case, drinking would only spoil
your glossy pink lipstick and destroy your chances.

Boys in the sixties were courageous. As the band
started to play, they had to risk, one by one,
crossing the bare maple floor to the other side
of the hall, where girls stood in rows waiting,
and ask, *Can I have this dance Miss?*

His greatest dread was if she replied
I'm not dancing. It meant
that every other girl in rows waiting would respond
similarly, leaving him to slink off in humiliation
to hide in the Gents.

On seeing this happen often, I vowed
to dance with any boy, regardless
of looks. I kept my promise until one fateful night.
A not-so-handsome boy was refused
by the row of girls beside me.

I took his hand, stepped out on the dance floor.
The band played a jive, my favourite.
This didn't seem to be in his repertoire.
He tried to give me a twirl.
When I spun around, he had fallen to the floor.

Other dancers stepped back, left me
standing in my homemade mini-skirt, alone.
Two bouncers came to carry him off.
The refusers stood smiling from the sidelines.
I slunk to the Ladies, a new vow in mind.

On my way home early, a bouncer came over
to show me the naggin whiskey bottle
hidden in the boy's breast-pocket.
Dutch courage is dangerous when bouncing on maple.

Pádhraig

It is a long time ago since we borrowed
the row-boat, pushed off from the slipway,
jumped onto the cross-board.

I remember the dip and pull of the oars,
your arm muscles flexing each time you leaned
forward to carry us across the lake.

Together we dragged the boat onto the island bank,
searched for a sitting place under a tree,
its trunk wide enough for both our backs.

On that summer's evening, nestled together,
we listened to the water and birdsong
without a word between us.

Your young arm around my shoulder –
a sixteen-year-old
who knew how to hold my loss.

There was no birdsong, no rustle of trees
in the graveyard, only the thud of my mother's coffin
touching stone when the men let go.

Now, Charon has carried *you* across the Styx.
You have paid the price,
leaned into the place unknown,

where there are no words,
where my arm cannot reach
to comfort you, my friend.

Joan

He handed me the box marked *FRAGILE,*
offered to keep it for me if I preferred.
I took it in my arms, kissed the lid,
saying, *No.*

Your remains will have a home here
until Spring when we will climb
to Queen Maeve's feet and let the wind take you,
ash and bone,

up and out, to spread yourself free.
Free, not fragile, out to sea and sky
landing where you will.
What remains?

The you, that you were –
child girl, who whacked the dentist
when he hit a nerve.
Fiery fighter.

Wild teenager who mitched class,
caught in the act, laughing.
Risk-taker, hitch-hiker,
globe trotter,

kibbutz worker on a conveyer belt,
splitting plastic chairs with a hatchet.
Woman, afraid of getting in a rut.

Woman, generous-hearted, painter,
writer, questioner, ready to rage
for the voiceless, braver than me.
Not fragile.

Will-maker, wanting what you wanted.
Gifter of treasured possessions – mother's
precious wrist watch for me, worn without working
always on your arm;

the lost Belleek Christening cup
found, forty years later,
promised to your special
god-daughter;

a copper kettle with a hidden letter inside
for your friend Gary,
words for him only
after your death.

Your Indian Jewellery box; diamond rings,
and miraculous medals
for the cousin you trusted
to support you during those last months.

My heart is torn.
There is no out of this.
It owns me.
I could fall into it like a fledgling

who throws caution to the wind,
allows the sky to rule its destiny –
a risk that may take me down
into the abyss

where I fear forgetfulness lives.

Grandma

My mouth begins to pucker now
just like my grandmother's upper lip.

I used to look at her and wonder
how skin could turn to withered paper.

I didn't know it took years of hearty
laughter, coy smiles, pouting at suitors,

determination to finish every job
before going to bed. That it was a mouth

set in pride at a job well done,
breathing hard to birth her child,

silenced when she wanted to scream.
A mouth that had grimaced at grim sights,

trembled in fear
when the IRA held her hostage.

A mouth that mumbled rosaries for loss of her beloved,
collapsed in disappointment, sang tearfully

when her grandchild played on the piano,
The Last Rose of Summer.

Extremes

We stand on the razored edge of Benbulben,
viewing St. John's Point and Raughley at our feet.
We've climbed Cúchulainn's table,
wind tangle-dancing our hair
as we goat-step in zig-zag along scree slopes.

We pose for a group photo at the ridge
overlooking the corrie and lake below.
Standing at Sruth in Aghaidh an Aird
we marvel at the notion of a stream
flowing upwards in winter winds.

Before we make our way down
Swiss valley to bathe our feet
in Glencar lake, our leader moves nearer
the precipice for a panoramic shot.

With each of his steps I lurch and gasp.
It becomes a game, he steps backward,
I reach out in terror,
my heart pounding.

Everyone laughs.
He takes the picture.
With no idea that I am going over the edge
again and again with my dead sister.

Mushroom

There was the continuous
shsh… shsh… shsh…
of the ocean
pounding in the background,
but my focus came down
to a small thing:
one mushroom sprouting
in the sand.

I wondered
what gave it sustenance.
How remarkable
it could hold me.
More spectacular
than the dunes
or sand-floor of shells or sky
or pain that gnaws at loss.

Just This

The vague loneliness
comes at times
when there is a blue breeze
in cool sun;

between work-time and tea-time;
on the way to the sea;
just after eating;
sometime before sleep.

A slight stir
with a tinge of longing,
it occupies a small space
below the breast bone.

A card from my aunt with an image of migrants picking cockles in Morecambe Bay

I can only see their bent backs,
the strain of spine to the task,
picking from sand
the catch,
each one alone, gathering.

Just that they look like hollow wraiths
in a triangle of falling sun
at the edge of a sky.
I expect them to fade,
absorbed into the sand they forage.

You sent me this card as a thank you
for giving you back the past –
anger (eighty years on)
towards habited women
who hurt you, in the name of God.

You want to have your say
in the copperplate writing
they taught you,
while there is still light.

Two Sisters (On the Terrace)

Pierre-Auguste Renoir

Reunion is only a motion away,
a sound, a song, the rhythms
of Bob Dylan *Knocking on Heaven's Door,*

Lara's Theme on a re-run of *Dr. Zhivago,*
a postcard on the mat from some foreign city,
the stride of a woman walking ahead,

making you rush to catch up until
the shock, knowing you have forgotten
in that glanced moment.

Such is loss. Unspoken out of fear
that you will be seen as unhinged.
Years she's been gone. Yes.

Years, months, days and hours.
No matter. In that momentary reunion,
the heart still pounds with longing.

The Visit

You're very good to come.
Reclining in her purple chair,
she praises her son for buying it,
sometimes calls him 'Patrick'
(her husband's name).

The room is deadly quiet,
other residents doze or sleep
in their common-or-garden seats,
occasionally calling out *Nurse, nurse,*
eyes still closed.

In the room opposite
a man is playing keyboard.
Tunes from the '40s and '50s.
I ask if she likes the music –
What music?

I used to bring homemade treats,
a china cup, flask of strong tea.
Now, I hold a plastic beaker
to her lips. Sometimes she gags,
even on water.

I reach out to hold her hand,
stroke it gently. We sit together,
apart in this strange world.
'The heart has its reasons
that reason cannot understand.'

Her eyes close.
On my way out, I fill in the mandatory
Visitors Book – Date, Resident visited,
Time of Departure.
I ask the nurse for the Exit code.

Mary

May is your month, rosaries and hymns,
a golden month. You are the queen
of whins and whitethorn stars.
My mother prayed to you
and to your mother too.

She had a saint for every pregnancy,
a name for every child,
a mother-of-pearl prayer book
filled with novena cards –
intercessionaries who carried petitions
on her behalf to God.

She had her *Nine Fridays*,
her lay Franciscan order,
a simple brown habit for her shroud,
a belief as big as her delight
in style and friends and dances.
Hope as wide as Mullagh strand
where she swam breaststroke
in the tide each summer.

A talent for creating apple tart;
queen cakes with jam and cream;
a penchant for Battenberg
wrapped in marzipan;
Sunday's speciality her sherry trifle.

A determination to have Mass
celebrated in the new house
against Parish rules, even if it meant
lacing the canon's tea with brandy.
Always her John Player's untipped
held between first and second fingers,
nails painted in pink polish,
a wash-and-set on Saturdays.

The children bathed before bedtime,
pipe-cleaners for curls in their hair,
fasting from teatime 'til next noon,
best frocks laid out and shoes
shone for Sunday.

A woman innocent and faithful,
trusting like you, Mary, the mother of mothers.
In her final month, wheelchair bound,
she made her way to Lourdes,
took the baths, touched the Grotto wall.

Elegy

There are no flowers on your plot.
Some plant fuchsia, red roses into clay,
others leave grass to grow green.

Yours is cemented down
among rows of polished granite,
etched names, dates of death.

Only nineteen years old, Frankie.
Concrete and stone can't stop
you breaking through.

Witnessing

I light a white candle for each of you,
for innocence, for loss.
I light a red candle for myself,
for blood,
for my Gethsemane.

White for your Golgotha,
for the quietness when you speak,
for the childhood that is gone.
Red for tears we owe ourselves,
for screams you held inside.

White for you who took the blame
to save the younger ones.
White for the fight to continue,
for fragments of hope, for truth.

A genuflection to honour
the Calvary we have walked,
for every word of your struggle to tell.
White for the trust it has taken.

Red for courage and pain,
for sorrow,
light for witnessing, for tomorrow,
for your children and their children
who now have the power of saying
NO.

The Hour Glass

After the shootings in Las Vegas 1.10.2017

Each grain-drop is time enough for change,
a whole life-fall from music to silence.
Sounds of celebration, fireworks become gunshot,
in one grain-drop, in a party city.

Each grain-drop, enough time to wound, to kill.
Each grain-drop a bullet of anger released,
a hate fire, firing murder, loaded and re-loaded.
Rat-tat-tat, sand drops,
bodies falling, moans and shock gasps,
terror and running.

Each particle an end, a loss of being human.
Every bullet whizz an emptying,
a tearing into limbs, into hearts.
A last bullet for the assassin.

We are here, far away, watching the grains
that have fallen in minutes from the upper glass
to the lower, emptied.

Cleave

A crossword puzzle
can open your eyes
to words,
sounds,
the strangeness of meaning,
contradiction.
Cleave:
come apart, sever.
And its opposite –
Cleave:
cling to, adhere.

A dictionary tries to do justice.
There is none,
neither in severance
nor in holding on.
Antonyms or synonyms
only complicate
the pain
when you have fallen apart,
become two halves
separated by life
or a surgeon's knife.

Your heart, unable,
disabled,
clings to the story
over and over
while you stir the pot,
rhubarb jam
adhering to the sides,
waiting
for the point
of wrinkle to set
on a cold saucer.

There was just the delve,
elbowing out,
the push,
nothing left
to reach
and touch.
Only
the word
to tell you:
cleave to.
You are cleaved from.

Christine

Keeler, Profumo, Ward and Me

Christine, were you an innocent or a fool?
Searching for father always.
Choosing fun as freedom. Going down
blind alleys where old men led you.

Christine, beautiful and naïve,
wild rebellion in your heart,
desperate to be seen, to be heard
by anyone who would listen.

Unaware that the powerful have
all the cards when it comes down to truth
or lies. The *Swinging Sixties* were to set you free
from dead-end jobs, from poverty.

Not a nine-month prison sentence
for perjury, although that man beat you
black and blue.
Over and over.

The only man who made you feel safe
abandoned life and you.
His high-flying friends
used you both, even when you said:

I'm not a tart, not a prostitute,
not a victim. Who were you then?
Scapegoated like your saviour
Dr. Ward, osteopath, artist.

He offered you for fun,
for free to politicians, lords
and gentlemen until you were
on your knees, scrubbing prison floors
while they disowned you from their foreign villas.

Did all the tabloids do you favours,
selling you for gain? Content to condemn you
when the time was right for profit.

Oh Christine! For all they vilified you
and all your foolishness, you gathered
your cash, kept your promise
to buy a semi for your mum.

Mother, father, men, they took from you.
You gave willingly. Did fame make you free
when they took and took and gave you little back?
Not even a kind word.

Final Gallows

in memory of Michael Manning (1929–1954) and
Catherine Cooper (1888–1953)

Michael's memory of the night is alcohol-erased.
Proven guilty as charged,
his cap at the scene, evidence enough.

On her everyday walk home from nursing the sick,
Catherine's body is ravaged.
There is no mercy for her.

There is no mercy for him.
A year too early
for his life to be spared.

Although he moves meekly without resistance,
they walk him, one at each elbow,
to the appointed place.

Hooded, inside that room, they stand him
on the fatal floorboard and expertly
slip the noose over his head.

Brisk as an eyeblink without thought,
the trapdoor swings with one loud bang
echoing in the eight-foot fall.

His young body
is carried to an unmarked
Mountjoy prison grave.

Above the Below

David Blaine's 44-day incarceration in a
plexiglass box suspended over the Thames close
to Tower Bridge, London, in 2003

A painting in the Appleloft gallery
looks like a figure inside a glass box.

The owner assures me it isn't the man
who hung over London for weeks.

I am already caught up in reverie, alone
in the sky, within the glass box, feeling

too hot, too cold, how not to give up,
how not to go mad.

Rain streaking my cube window
like tears. Taking the flak from below:

workmen's gall; spectacle for the bored;
crick in the neck to passers-by.

I am above all that, concerned with choice –
how much water to drink; peeing in public;

the length of light; cloud shadows; dark
covering me – and fear. Remembering poems,

reciting what I can, struggling for images, faces,
friends who might get me through,

family who probably won't. My skin sweat-damp,
length of fingernails, toenails – tearing them off.

Lowered to ground, my glass cage opens.
Hands lift me onto the stretcher. Siren screams.

Below the Above now,
I look up and learn

that neither sky nor earth
can heal this void of loneliness.

Wild Grief

After the Pietà by Michelangelo

She holds him across her lap,
laden with his dead weight. You can feel the burden,
the strength of her will to support her son,
adoration holding her up.

His face lost in faraway seeing,
hers, beatific in sorrow and knowing.
Knowing not the future, only past joy and pain.

They are one being, flowing between spirit.
Her loss of him, a death – his death, a living light
shining out in silent testimony.
Her own self disappeared into hope for humanity,
her gaze of love poured out through him to you and you.

In awe, I look from the crown of her head and veil,
to shoulders, breast and raptured arms,
down to Christ's bruised face and languid limbs,
the folds of her cloak, her knees through marble fabric,
as she surrenders to the wild grief of a mother,
the heartbreak.

Bridget's Cross

I spot them:
lush green rushes
on the way to Hazelwood.
I pluck the longest ones
with least brown tips.

I fold each stem
to face north, east, south and west,
overlap, tuck in,
hold to trim and tie.

I show you
there are many ways
of making love.

A Room

There are many rooms in my Father's house

John lived in one room
after his sister died.
Rats lived there too.
They didn't bother each other.
John foraged, found a tree,
cut and dragged it with chains
into his room, fed it
bit by bit to the fire.

A rose grew inwards
through his broken window,
flowered by firelight.
A kettle sat on the burning tree,
John boiled water for tea
and liver for his dinner.
Liver-water made strong tea.

A neighbour woman brought
a cooked meal every day.
He fed it to the rats. John wasn't
a charity case, he had the key
to his freehold property.

When grass in the chimney pot
grew roots, when slates fell off,
when his Poitín ran out
the rats moved out, no-one came for tea.
His neighbour stopped bringing dinners.

He took the District Nurse's word
of a better place with warmth and safety.
He lived six months in a room without rats,
a dry bed and the company of strangers.

In a church without hymns, a handful
of mourners, a decent burial
was paid for by the woman who got
his half acre in return for weekly visits
to the County Home.

A Floorboard Speaks as Metaphor

It is good to be hugged close,
to lay side by side
flat out among friends,
to share all we have in common,
stretched to our limits.

A community supporting one another,
open to receive the footprint
of all who need to pass over us,
to welcome outsiders and insiders,
to hear whispers and shouts
without comment.

We keep our ears close to the ground
all day long, all life long,
while we are here,
quietly accepting
the imprint of others.

Lament for Bertie

Animal companion 2000-2016

There will be no more twirls on the dunes,
tail held high, headed for home,
eager for after-walk treats.

His little life is over. His leash lies idle
on the table. His fireside cushion
no longer holds his warm body.

No more belly rubs or strokes
on the soft fur of his head and ears.
Our chocolate-box Bertie is gone.

No more sharp barks in the back of the van
nor after dinner, for his rightful share of leftovers.
No more barks when he wants out and in again.

No waking in the night and at first light.
He won't see the skylark rise this Spring
nor the stonechats hop from post to post.

He won't hear the cuckoo call
nor the stream flow
beneath his earthen bed.

The sunset blazed gold and red this evening.
Red for love and sorrow.
Gold for joy.

The Island of Pigs

Inish Corkish, Upper Lough Erne

An island of trees where striped pigs shade
on summer days, fattening on herbs and wildflowers.
They hear the uncommon curlew sing
and new frogs croak.
They own the place and the island owns them.

These pigs, like sumo wrestlers
wear a black belt around their fat bellies.
They waddle and snort as they forage,
content with every morsel of treasure.
They are family, generation after generation.

This is an island of innocence where warm waters ripple
on the lake surface, where graceful reeds
hold a glimpse of swans. The pigs know the farmer
as their friend. He rows across from the mainland,
pats their plump heads as he counts.

He counts his notes at market,
disconnected from the dissonance
of gun, knife and slab, the selection
of black pig bacon on Darling Street
for the housekeeper's pan.

An Daingean

There are humps and hollows
in the road
between Dingle and Tralee,
Mount Brandon black
and overhung with intermittent grey.

I round a turn
to turquoise streaks of sea.

At Annascaul bluebells
purple in the ditch,
gorse scents of coconut
through the open window.

No dolphin in Dingle today,
a cloudburst cancels
the hourly boat trips.
On the salt-tiered pier
I meet a young man
with a head-full of curls,

streaks of light
in his dancing eyes.
He activates the lift
from his electric wheelchair
gliding onto the ramp
of his minibus.

The stronghold of his smile
holds mine as he says
*This day was nearly worth
breaking my neck for.*

Going to the Island

Drive into the moon,
full-faced – just a sliver licked
from her cream forehead.
The Great Bear cradling light
against black rain, tar and night.

Steer through Clogher and Augher
as she veers east and west, sometimes
head-on along the motorway, Belfast
beating on our windscreen.

Sleep in the moon,
drifting to the whizz of traffic
like midnight breath that rises and fades
on Cavehill.

Dream in the moon,
cheek to cheek with her watery smile,
dance the dark night 'til she dies.

Take off into the sky and disappear
until dawn is a purple band on the horizon,
plane wheels touching you down.

Reading Poems

I give you my thumping heart,
the tightness in my breath.

I give you my voice to keep.
Its fear of being lost,
choked out in gulps
for one last word.

Fear of losing myself without words,
of there being no me –

no poem, no way of saying
and you not hearing
what I need to tell you.
How it is, where it is,
so I am not alone
anymore.

Meditation

Did my heart speak or my mind?
Did my heart listen as my mind spoke?
Did my heart feel the light rather than my eye see it?
Was my heart sending love
to the bird and the branch she sat upon?
Was my heart aflame, open to the unfamiliar?
Was my heart a bird's song,
a cat purring, a catkin on a stem?

Did my heart bare itself
to the wetness of rain?
Will my heart heal all the questions
I have no answer for? Will my heart know how?
Will other hearts show me?
Will I allow them?

Nevermore (O Taiti)
Paul Gauguin 1897

My dear master
I will lie here, feign smiles
while you desire
my toes, curling,
my hips, curving,
my nipples, proud.

I do as I'm told
because you,
older,
chose me
over the other
girls.

You can paint
my beauty,
dark and light.

My soul
is in the birds.
My song
is in the sun.
My heart
flows in the sea.

Flowers
adorn my life.
In cool shade
every tree
wraps her green arms
above my head.

My baby
is washed
into the earth.

Blue and lemon
taint my body.

Portrait

Not for you, a day without graces,
angry faces, land-locked places,
cheering masses, smart-asses,
keep-fit classes.

Not for you, cheaters, chasers,
gamblers, racers, match-makers,
baulkers, stalkers, power-walkers,
fast-talkers.

Not for you, all-nighters, always-righters,
take-you-down-a-peg-or-two-ers,
bullies, bouncers, keep-you-outers.

Not for you, begrudgers, judgers,
the moneyed, honeyed property-
developers, end-of-the-world-
is-nigh-ers

who don't see the stars, the moon,
birds in flight and song, the honey-bee,
the light of our lives, love that shines
in darkness.

Digging

after Seamus Heaney

Going down, down for the good word,
the one that says it right in this flickering moment,
the one that nicks and slices to truth.
Cut into the deep sedge.
Its cold hardness takes the coarse shaft
of pain remembered,
forty years away, buried since.

Levered out and up, rasping in curt cuts
as you stoop to heave memory
over the edge of yesterday.
Peel away layers between finger and thumb
to raw nakedness, nestled inside
the rhythms of forgetfulness.

You sit now in the space dug out
with a word that doesn't fit
until you hear the voices of Magdalenes
their harrowing stories told.
Suffering, tall and wild in daylight.

After Reading Christina Rossetti's *Up-Hill*

Those who have gone before know the way
but cannot show us the road.

They don't watch or wait for us,
their journey done.

We scramble, trip and tumble,
learn that graze is intrinsic to being whole.

Accepting there is no easy route.
This, the miracle bequeathed.

Our guide, a day's sunlight.
Sustenance among friends.

The only clue, the roar of the ocean
somewhere in the distance.

Eucalyptus

Rising tall and upright, taller
than I can lean back to see
full-height; filtered by light.
Rising, straight as a die
from soft green undergrowth.

Stripped back to pale bark,
shed like snakeskin,
hanging from white tree frames.
Every breath I take
is menthol-fresh.

This is Fatima, cool and sunny,
a holy place, quiet in February
where three young shepherdesses
tended their flock,
unknowing of the world's wounded ways.

Ears only for angels, eyes to see sun-dance
and vision, voices only for a woman's words,
time for rosary and shepherding.
Their stories disbelieved a hundred years ago,
in a time of war, a time of lies and killing.

Today, there is a village, statues and stations,
cathedral and cross, candles burning at the grotto,
medals, Masses and a museum, blessed children,
their short lives named on headstones:
Francisco and Jacinta. Lucia left alone to carry the mystery.

But my eye is for the eucalyptus
standing straight as a die,
bare as truth, holding the secret of Fatima,
finding its way towards the light.

Terminus

Last rose petals fallen have deep peach perfume.
Firm in my hand an apple is stolen from birds.
Autumn brambles have shrivelled blackberries.
Deora Dé, tears of God: the final fuchsia bells hang limply.
Tree trunks lie severed in the field –
might their root source regrow or die?
The clock ticks a constant heartbeat.
Feet hold the floor above the earth.
Weeds know best how to grow.
A chime tolls sweetly as I pass under its spell.
My name is on the list for ending.

Gift

At times, we have stayed quietly
in our own silences
letting the sun reign,
the wind sing her lament,
allowing the cold its timing.

Giving attention to the robin
who robs the pyracantha berries
to feed his bright red belly.
Giving sympathy when the blackbird
steals the bigger share.

Receiving daylight and darkness equally.
Receiving words from a Tagore poem,
pondering them until a spark of connection
renews our faith and hope
in the variety that shapes the universe.

Receiving this time, this place,
this transient, intangible wholesomeness
that we offer each other
with arms wide open to possibility.

Time to Remember

It is time to be, to listen
for the sedge warbler warning us
from his residence
among willow.

It is time to remember what gives joy –
the cat's mad rush through the flap
and her wild flight up the apple tree
to harass a robin.

Time to listen again to Mozart's *Requiem*
on a wet morning while the wind
shakes the violet blossom
from the Solanum bush

as the kettle sings for tea
and bananas ripen on the window sill,
warm, softening.
Time to remember.

Remember picnics by the river –
lapwings who tumble-dive and climb
to avert the hunting heron. Dragonflies,
hovering light as air above water.

Remember again the twist and bends
through marram, ruby marsh orchids
in the dunes as you wend towards sea.
Flawless swans floating on the lake.

Remember the delight
in glimpses of reed bunting
through bulrush and yellow flag iris.
Time to remember.

Time to hear your own feet,
your very own heartbeat.
Time to learn this song is yours,
always throbbing.

What Is Shredded Within

for Lisa

You share fragments of a life,
spoken in syllables, disjointed
as a day, absorbed into night.

Your companion gone –
no animal fur to stroke.
She has left you, broken with age,
alone now in the morning, alone
in the night. Cold, very cold.

No point in harbouring sorrow, you say.
Your will or belief in the voice
that says *I am with you,*
I am with you, as you pull yourself out
of the drowning river, rise up to clutch
the branch, climb out to wade the mud bank,
shaking. Your eyes full with loss.

A book you wrote, lifts you into the sky;
a gannet's wing span above Skellig Michael;
one of Rilke's poems you can recite by heart.
Somehow, meaning enters through memory:
the vivid colours of a puffin painted wild;
remembered places, faces that lift you
like the branch you clung to that night.

You don't know how the shift came.
The pieces still in shreds but you make a friend
in this new home, where death holds hands,
where others' minds have disappeared.
This carer-friend who whispers
I'll put the heat on,
when you shiver.

Where Do Poems Come From?

when you're not sure
whether it was the Chicken
Dhansak last night or the half
bottle of Chilean you had
with it or that time of month –
a moonful of lunacy
that makes your stomach queasy
in bed, when you curl, turn from side
to side, toes out, then in; lie on your back;
try face down; all fours; too hot you throw
the quilt off, too cool you pull it on again;
try a lighter one from the hot-press,
fold it in two; get up, walk about,
lie down; don't disturb your lover
from his doze; lift a dead-weight arm
from across your breast; anything
but sleep.